Moving

Written by Helen Depree • Illustrated by Bob Kerr

"Here comes a big truck,"
said Grandma.

2

3

"Here come two big children," said Sharma.

4

5

The men carry in the bed.
The children carry in the chair.

Dad carries in the table.

"Hello," said Grandma
to the children.
"I am Grandma
and this is Sharma
and this is Jake
and this is Patch."

"I am Tommy,"
said Tommy,
"and this is Sam
and this is Dad
and this is Tabby."

12

13

"Come in and have some cake,"
said Grandma to Dad and the children.